Keep

MW01488574

SIMPLE
THINGS

This book would never have seen the light of day without my wife Meredith. She was my main inspiration and source of encouragement and support. I think back on the past 10 years since this book's conception, there were so many times I quit on this project and she wouldn't let me. She would gently remind me to, "Remember your book." In addition to providing all the beautiful artwork, she also authored many of the "Simple Things" I lift my chalice to her!

Simple Things

Print ISBN: 978-1-7354338-0-6
ebook ISBN: 978-1-7354338-1-3

Artwork by: Meredith E. Schuster-Gansrow
www.meredithartist.com
Instagram: @meredithartist22/

Printed in the United States

CONTENTS

Kinesthesia and Touch	9
Taste	73
Smell	99
Sight	143
Sound	179
Mind	213
All Senses Involved	315

Simple Things lifts the spirits and feeds the soul while tickling the imagination and energizing all of the senses. This book invites us to recapture the joy of seeing the world with eyes of love and childlike wonder and encourages us to shine brightly with the inner spark of eternal love that illuminates us all.

–Cynthia Sue Larson, author of *Reality Shifts & Quantum Jumps*

In Simple Things, the reader is offered a menu of exceptionally simple ways to open the way for a lifepath of mindfulness and gratitude. Using the five senses to expand awareness and appreciation, this guide shows the reader how to live what Zorba the Greek calls "the full catastrophe of life." In these troubling times, the practice outlined in Simple Things can make a world of difference.

–Laurie Nadel, Ph.D., author of *The Five Gifts: Discovering Hope, Healing and Strength When Disaster Strikes*

When Mike first came to me with his idea for Simple Things I couldn't even imagine it as a full book. I guess in my mind it was so, well, too simple. As he began writing I found the book idea contagious. Ultimately it inspired the artwork you see intermittently throughout the pages.

I truly believe that creativity does not belong to a select few. Creativity is one of the most beautiful aspects of being human and it is a right given to us all. We simply choose to,(or not) tap into its amazing gifts. We all have different forms of expression but it's all there. May you find your muse and enjoy one of the best ways to feel more alive. Simple Things did that for me and it is with hope that Simple Things will do that for you too.

-Meredith

Simple Things is a book of appreciation and gratitude. My wish for you is that the Simple Things will act as a catalyst for positive mindset and change.

In the practice of observing Simple Things on a regular basis, you can begin to deeply appreciate life in full, including its vicissitudes. Immersing yourself in the Simple Things, you will begin to notice more and organically grow in mindfulness. This will set a course for seeking out more transformative tools for growth and harmony.

As each Simple Thing transforms into a unique and separate meditation, you will come to see the extraordinary in the ordinary.

The Simple Things are meditations on everyday experiences that often escape our consciousness in the reality of our increasingly technology-focused world. These meditations help us to focus our attention on the present moment, on life's simple pleasures, and on fostering deeper connections with ourselves, our loved ones, and our world. I was inspired to write these meditations as a way of tapping into the universal life source that simply requires us to be present in our mind, body, and spirit—no devices needed.

My intention is for you, the reader, to savor each Simple Thing. There is no need to rush—please enjoy each experience as an independent meditation. If one especially resonates with you, remain with it for as long as you like. Engage as many senses as possible—this will enhance your experience of each Simple Thing. When you are satisfied with your experience of a Simple Thing, feel free to move on to another one. Try to take note of which Simple Things resonate with you most deeply. If you are inspired to create something—a drawing or a painting, or a song if music is your bag—then the Simple Things have offered you something valuable. Simple Things are meant to be taken slowly. Drink them in and share them so someone else may also benefit. You may even be inspired to write your own Simple Things.

Enjoy the journey, and remember to notice the Simple Things in your daily life. Anyone could have written these: a five-year-old child understands these concepts. The Simple Things are all around us. We only have to take the time to pause, notice, and appreciate them.

I have attempted to distill these meditations down to their barest essence because I want readers to be able to derive their own meanings from them. They will evoke different things for different people because we each see the world through our own unique prism. It's very important to me that I not influence you by stating my individual interpretations of the Simple Things. It is my hope that you will find meaning, understanding, and value in each Simple Thing on your own. By just taking a brief moment each day to notice the Simple Things, the more complex parts of life will become easier. Simple Things bring you back to that quiet place inside of yourself that we often seem to lose track of during the hustle and bustle of everyday existence. Through the practice of observing Simple Things on a regular basis, you will develop a deeper appreciation for life and all its vicissitudes. You will see the extraordinary in the ordinary.

Kinesthesia and Touch

A good laugh.

A walk on the beach.

Slow walks in a serene place.

Shooting baskets.

Knitting a sweater.

Rolling the sand between your toes.

Sitting under your favorite shady tree.

Taking a yoga class on a Saturday morning.

Hotel luxury shower heads.

Playing in the rain.

Lounging in a comfortable pair of sweatpants.

A bubble bath.

A great long shower with no time limit. A tub big enough to lie down in.

Falling asleep at the beach.

Making a snow angel.

Lying on a really comfortable mattress with lots of extra pillows.

Laughing until your belly hurts.

Cool sheets on a muggy night.

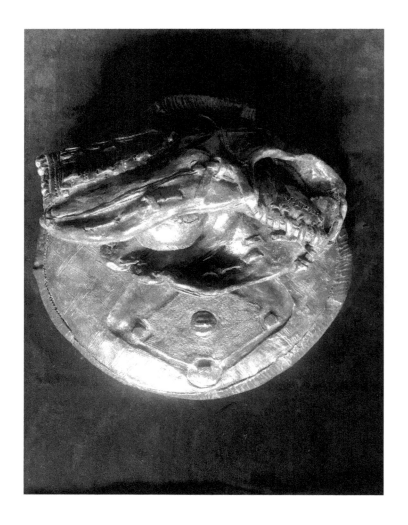

Having a baseball catch.

Walking on unused train tracks.

Picking and eating blueberries from the bushes in summer.

Going outside in your bathing suit during a
sun shower.

Getting a relaxing massage.

A lick on the face from a puppy.

Comforting a child.

Holding hands with someone you love.

Catching a dandelion and making a wish.

Holding a child's hand.

Holding a sleeping baby.

Petting a dog.

Soothing a baby to sleep.

Taste

A delicious meal.

Hot cocoa after shoveling snow.

Ice cream on a warm summer evening.

Slowly sipping tea and feeling it go down
your throat.

A picnic in a meadow or park.

A snowflake caught on your tongue.

A slice of pizza from a
New York City pizzeria.

Eating fried chicken at the beach.

Homemade pie at a roadside diner.

Discovering a new restaurant in your city or town.

The first bite of a juicy peach in season.

Getting a free sample of your favorite treat.

Smell

The smell of fresh towels.

Coming home to freshly baked brownies.

Clothing sun-dried on a clothesline.

The smell of brilliant, green, freshly cut grass.

A stack of clean and fresh-smelling laundry.

Giving or receiving flowers.

Baking cookies for children.

Inhaling the sea air on an early summer morning.

The wonderful aroma of hot honey-roasted
peanuts from a vendor's cart on
a cool evening.

Coffee brewing in the morning.

New car smell.

The smell of a freshly printed dittoed copy
(for those who remember).

A Christmas tree.

The way a baby smells.

Freshly cooked bacon.

Fresh air.

Coconut.

Burning wood.

Morning dew in the countryside.

Your favorite essential oils used in a
restorative yoga session.

The enticing smell of freshly baked bread as you walk by a bakery in the early morning.

Sight

A smile on a child's Face.

Unexpectedly finding your favorite movie on TV.

A pretty sunset.

Finding an old photo that you like.

Making pictures out of clouds, observing cloud animals.

Watching the sunr_se.

Seeing your children tucked into bed.

Receiving a handwritten love letter.

Seeing a rainbow.

Watching a flock of birds flying in a pattern.

Watching a candle burn.

The sight of mountains at the peak of fall.

Watching a horse run.

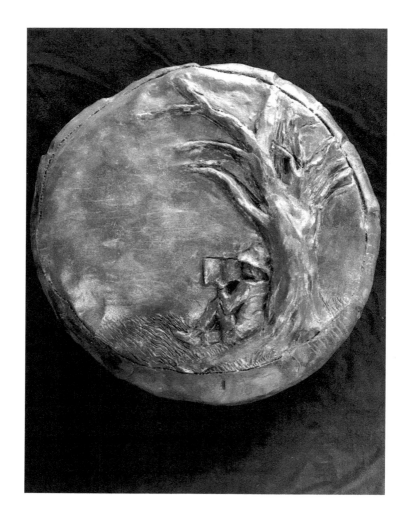

Reading a book under a shady tree
in summer.

Seeing a deer on an early morning jog or walk.

Drive-in movies on clear, star-filled nights.

Finding a $10 bill in your newly washed
pants.

Sound

A nice song.

Hearing a cat purr.

Listening to someone play guitar at a campfire.

The hum of a well-tuned car engine.

Listening to a transistor radio.

Finding a beloved concert by your favorite band or performer on YouTube.

Waking up to birds chirping after a good
night of sleep.

Taking the time to listen to someone.

Receiving an uplifting text message.

Grooving with your favorite song on a great pair of headphones.

Hearing the cicadas buzz in the summer.

The sound of happy children playing.

The chirping of birdsong.

Village church bells on a sunny morning.

A waterfall.

Silence.

Mind

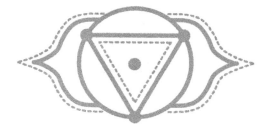

A sincere compliment.

A beautiful memory.

Solitude—"alone time."

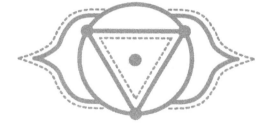

Quality time with a friend.

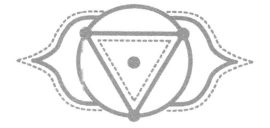

Graciously helping someone in need.

A quiet and peaceful mind.

A restful night's sleep.

A late afternoon nap.

Reconnecting with an old friend or loved one.

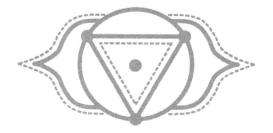

Giving to charity and not telling anyone
about it.

Thinking and remaining in a positive frame of mind when it would have been easy to go negative.

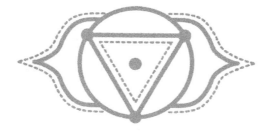

Not having to do anything.

Studying opposites.

Thinking of palindromes.

Quietly meditating, even for just
a few minutes.

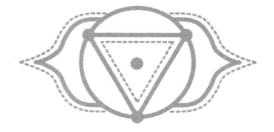

Taking time to pay it forward (fill in the action).

Making a new friend.

Thinking of oxymorons.

Saying hello with a hearty smile.

Taking the road less traveled.

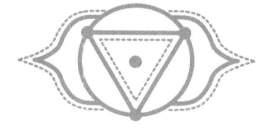

Love of country

Paying your bills early while thinking about
all that you have.

Mourning a loss with all your heart.

Just smiling.

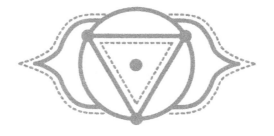

Writing a letter of gratitude.

Receiving a random act of kindness.

Getting lost in a book.

Discovering something new.

Being happy about a loved one's achievement.

Learning from the mistakes of others.

Writing a poem for your loved one.

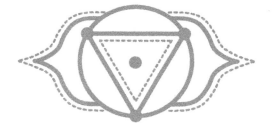

Feeling understood

The way you feel after rocking a baby to sleep.

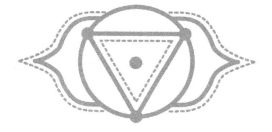

Welcoming new neighbors.

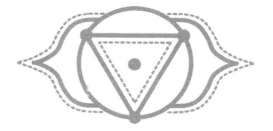

Visiting someone sick.

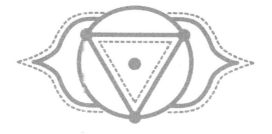

Crying when you're sad.

Sharing something you enjoy.

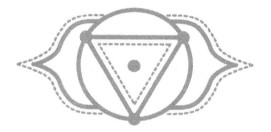

Fully accepting and owning your feelings
when something doesn't go your way.

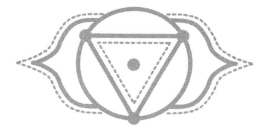

Spending time with friends.

Sending a postcard home.

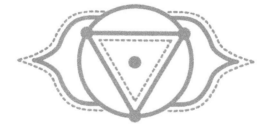

Daydreaming.

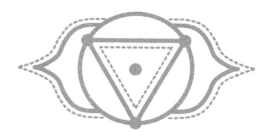

Crying when you're happy.

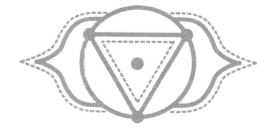

Finding joy in your life.

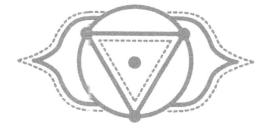

Contemplating the joy you've brought to others.

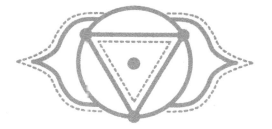

Doing good because it's the right thing to do.

The feeling you get when you've been brave.

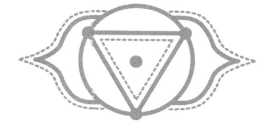

Getting lost in the Sunday New York Times crossword puzzle.

Practicing the Golden Rule.

Getting together with an old friend.

Breathing.

All Senses Involved

Just being.

Going for a long drive without a destination.

Walking your dog on a quiet moonlit night.

Growing and tending a garden.

Road trips that take you away.

Exploring a new place.

Subway rides.

Getting lost in a corn maze on an early autumn day.

County fairs.

Walking on a crisp autumn evening.

Being "in the zone."

Finding a gift you made as a child for someone you loved.

Taking a spontaneous trip.

Lying in a hammock on a cool summer evening.

Toasting marshmallows at a campfire.

Catching and releasing fireflies with your children on a warm summer evening.

The feeling you get when the first signs of spring appear—the buds on the trees.

Feeding ducks in a pond.

Searching for four-leaf clovers.

The first signs of autumn.

Fresh new snow.

Working on a project when everyone else is asleep.

Getting a gift in the mail.

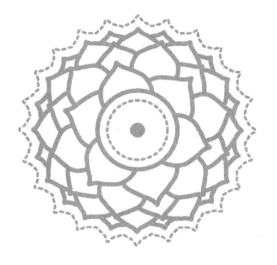

A cozy movie marathon with a loved one on
a winter Sunday.

Going for a nature walk and encountering
wildlife.

Getting up in the morning.

The reuniting of a great band.

Sitting around a warm firepit with friends.

Weather that turns for the better.

Watching and listening to the tide roll in, and
then watching and listening to it roll out.

A brand new shirt.

The quiet of the morning when no one else is awake.

Getting a gift in the mall.

Taking in a baseball game on a beautiful
late spring afternoon.

Writing your own Simple Thing.

Author Bio

After obtaining his massage license in 1996, Michael Gansrow embarked on a career as a massage therapist. He then met his future wife while working together in the field and joined her in business doing chair massage at Colleges and Universities and corporations. He began a meditation and yoga practice in 2005 which started him on an inner journey to self-discovery. The process grew organically, and as it did he began to create these Simple Meditations. Mr. Gansrow lives in Long Island NY with his wife Meredith and 3 children. He enjoys playing guitar and harmonica and writing poetry.

CPSIA information can be obtained
at www.ICGtesting.com
Printed in the USA
FSHW021931280221
78998FS

Friendship Bracelet

How To Make Fun, Easy & Stylish Friendship Bracelets & Charms To Wear And Share!

By Cindy Neals

Table of Contents

Introduction: 1

Chapter 1: Friendship Bracelets 3

Chapter 2- Getting Started 9

Chapter 3 – Classic Friendship Bracelets 20

Chapter 4 – Wrapped Friendship Bracelets 51

Chapter 6 – Braided Friendship Bracelets 68

Chapter 7 – Tips on Making Friendship Bracelets 81

Conclusion: 87

INTRODUCTION:

Thank you for downloading **Friendship Bracelet:** How To Make Fun, Easy & Stylish Friendship Bracelets & Charms To Wear And Share!

This book is filled with loads of information on Friendship Bracelets and how to create these charming accessories.

Whether you're an expert on making bracelets or a beginner wanting to try your hand out at this craft, you'll certainly find something you can use in this book. From basic macramé style bracelets to beaded masterpieces, you have quite a few to choose from.

This book contains the following information:
- Origin of Friendship Bracelets
- Types of Friendship Bracelets
- Materials Needed to Make Friendship Bracelets
- Basic Knotting and Other Skills Needed
- Getting Started: Easy Friendship Bracelets

- How to Make Classic Friendship Bracelets;
  - 2 Strand
  - Candy
  - Chevron
  - Diamonds
  - Hearts
  - Alphabets
- How to Make Wrapped Friendship Bracelets
- How to make Braided Friendship Bracelets
- How to Make Classic Friendship Bracelets with Beads

CHAPTER 1: FRIENDSHIP BRACELETS

ORIGIN OF FRIENDSHIP BRACELETS

What is a Friendship Bracelet?

A friendship bracelet is an accessory that is widely popular among people of all ages. Nowadays, these can be purchased and worn to compliment one's outfit. It comes in a variety of patterns and colors that make it a fun and flexible accessory. It is often made of embroidery thread, which makes it quite versatile. And because of the type of material used, friendship bracelets are a popular beach accessory. You can often see folks swimming or doing other activities while wearing their friendship bracelets.

History of Friendship Bracelets

The origin of the friendship bracelet can be traced back to ancient times. The knotting technique used in most of the basic types of this bracelet is believed to have been invented by Indian tribes from the North, Central and South Americas. These tribes had a tradition of exchanging bracelets to symbolize their friendships.

The person who made the bracelet would put it on the wrist of the person they are giving it too. According to the custom, the bracelet should not be removed. The only time it could be taken off was when it got worn out on its own.

Keeping the bracelet on was a way to show appreciation for the time and effort spent making it as well as the friendship offered by the giver. Removing the bracelet when it was still in good condition was not a good thing. It meant that the friendship between the giver and the receiver had ended.

In the US, friendship bracelets were first seen in the 70's being worn in political rallies. Hippies took on the tradition of the Indian tribes and exchanged bracelets to symbolize brotherhood.

In the 80's this beautiful custom became popular among school kids and teenagers. During that time, dozens of kids could be seen laboring on bracelets that they would give their friends and loved ones.

The popularity of friendship bracelets have since grown. These are now worn even by older generations and aren't always handmade. With more and more people wearing this accessory, it is now readily available at stores. In addition, one doesn't even need to wait for other people to give it to them as it can now easily be purchased.

TYPES OF FRIENDSHIP BRACELETS

This charming accessory comes in different types. The classifications are based on the materials used as well as the manner in which the bracelets are created. Below are the popular kinds of friendship bracelets that you will learn how to make with this book,

1. Classic Friendship Bracelets – This is the most basic type of friendship bracelet that is made using macramé or knotting techniques. It is made from embroidery floss or thread, the same ones used for cross stitching. There are numerous patterns that can be created using the basic half knot,

    a. 2 Strand Friendship Bracelets – This is the simplest pattern to help you get started. It is made up of only two strands or sections and helps you get used to the 2 basic knots that you need to master. This is also a quick project to finish so you'll be able to see the end result in less than 10 minutes.

b. Candy Stripes - This playful pattern is the most common of all the friendship bracelet designs. This is of course because of how easy it is to make and how incredibly colorful the end result is. You could use as many colors as you want to create an eye catching design.

You can choose to create narrow stripes with only single rows for each color. You can also create thicker rows of color by simply arranging the order of the floss. The stripes pattern is a great way to enhance your knotting skills to prepare yourself for more intricate designs.

Popular stripe patterns include basic black and whites and other two toned contrasting colors. Holiday themes shades such as red and green for Christmas and orange and black for Halloween are quite common.

c. Chevron or Reversed V-Shaped – Named after the popular service station brand because the pattern closely resembles its logo. It is a more complex pattern than the basic stripes but still simple enough for a beginner to be able to create.

The chevron or reversed V- shaped pattern is perfect if you are looking for a bit more challenging project but still not quite ready for something time consuming.

d. Diamond – This pattern helps you add an interesting design to your bracelet. The diamond shapes create a unique look that resembles folk art designs which make it quite popular.

e. Custom Design – More experienced folks can create other interesting designs such as hearts and fish to adorn the bracelets they create for themselves and their loved ones.

Custom designs also include alphabet letters so friendship bracelets could display the name or initials of the wearer. Creating these involve following intermediate patterns but the end result is certainly one that you and your friends will enjoy.

2. Wrapped or Hippie Bracelets – As the name suggests, this type of friendship bracelet was popularized by hippies in the 70's. The peace loving folks handmade these accessories and exchanged it with each other. The exchange symbolized how they accepted each other as brothers and sisters.

Wrapped Friendship Bracelets often come in different colors and are quite easy to make as these do not require much knotting.

3.   Braided Friendship Bracelets – This type of bracelet is a great project as it doesn't use as much floss or thread as classic. It also has a few variations that look quite charming. The 3 strand or section braid is quick and easy to do and produces an attractive bracelet.

There are other more complex braids that utilize more strands that create interesting bracelets that will look professionally made even if you're just a beginner at this craft.

4.   Beaded Classic Friendship Bracelets - This type of accessory levels up the classic bracelet by adorning it with beads. It gives the design more depth and texture. You and your friends will certainly love wearing this charming bracelet.

CHAPTER 2- GETTING STARTED

MATERIALS NEEDED

Because there are different types of friendship bracelets that you can make, there are a variety of materials that you can use. Below is a quick reference of what you will need to prepare for your projects.

    a.   Embroidery Floss or Thread – You can choose from a multitude of colors available at craft stores t create the perfect bracelet.

    b.   Yarn – This type of yarn is great for alternative for cords for braided bracelets. They are cheap and can be found practically at any craft stores and even at your local supermarket.

To get the thickness you need though you will need to use at least three strands for each batch or section.

c. Safety Pins – Pins will come in handy in keeping the threads anchored while you are knotting. It is also the perfect to tool to unravel knots whenever you need to do it.

d. Buttons- While there are a lot of different ways to keep the bracelet fastened on the wrist, you'll find that using buttons can be

quite easy and convenient.

e.   Nylon string or nylon coated steel – this is
     the base material for your beaded bracelets
     so make sure that you choose the best
     quality you can find. Low quality strands
     may result in bracelets that may not be
     very durable.

f.   Beads – when making beaded friendship
     bracelets, the type of beads that you

choose is quite important. To make sure that you get the best color combinations, try to purchase your beads at the same time. If this is not possible, bring a sample of the beads that you will be using with the ones you are buying.

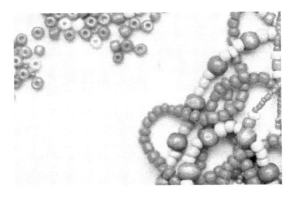

The size of your beads is also crucial. If the beads are too small, you might not be able to strand the nylon strings through. Also, while bigger beads may seem like a lot of fun, remember that these will also be a lot chunkier and may not be convenient to wear.

g. Clip Boards – This will let you continue making your bracelets even if you don't have a flat surface to work on. You can clip or tape the thread or yarn on to the board so you can easily make the knots and braids without the strands moving around too much.

h. Scissors – This is probably one of the most important equipment that you will need while making your bracelets. Make sure you have a pair of sharp medium sized scissors handy when working on your projects.

i. Tape – Packaging or masking tapes will work best. This will help you keep the bracelet in place closer to the sections that you are knotting or braiding to avoid any movements that may affect your pattern.

SKILLS NEEDED

While making the bracelets is a lot of fun, there are a few skills that you need to learn. These are skills that essential for you to be able to complete your projects. The succeeding chapters will give you a guide on how to make the specific style and pattern. These require being able to do the following,

Tying knots – classic friendship bracelets as mentioned in a previous section are a type of macramé. The patterns and the bracelets are made from tying knots. If the threads are not tied properly then the pattern might not come out right. You will then end up with wonky looking friendship bracelets.

1.   Below are the basic knots that you will be using,

        a.   Overhand Knot - This knot is used at the beginning and end of the bracelet. Using it at the beginning serves as an anchor to keep the embroidery thread or floss in place. Using it at the end locks the pattern or design and prevents your other knots from unraveling.

b. Forward Knot – This is one of the knots that will be creating your pattern. The knot will take the strand from the left to right. The

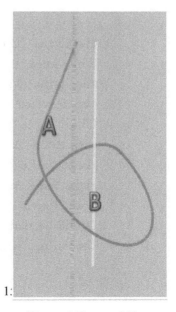

Figure 1 Forward Knot

color of the row that you will be creating with the forward knot is the same as the color of your active thread or floss.

When making a forward knot, the strand or section on the left is your active line while the one to its right is your standing line.

To create the knot, cross your active line over the standing line. This should create an outline with your strands that look like the number 4. Cross the active line under the standing line and pull it through the loop towards the left. When this is done, your active line should now be on the right side of your standing line

c. Backward Knot – This knot is tied the same way as the forward knot. The main difference is that the strand on your right hand side is your active string. It will be tied over the other strands

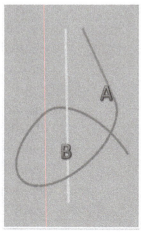

Figure 2 Backward Knot

16

so your active strand moves to the left.

When making a backward knot, the strand or section on the right is your active line while the one on the left is your standing line.

To create the knot, take your active line and cross it over your standing line. This should create an outline that resembles a reverse number 4. Cross the active line under the standing line and pull it through the loop to the right. Once this is done the active line is now to the left of your standing line.

d. Forward-Backward Knot – This knot will help you create more intricate designs for your bracelets as it combines the Forward Knot and Backward Knot so that it is tied on the same standing strand one after the other.

To create this knot, start with a forward knot. Once that is completed, take the same active string and do a backward knot. Your active line should be back to its starting position.

e. Backward Forward Knot – Just like the forward-backward knot, this type of knot is crucial when making bracelets with more complicated patterns such as alphabets and diamonds. This knot lets you do a backward and then forward knot on the same standing strand.

To create this knot, you first need to make a backward knot. Once you tighten the first knot, make a forward knot to take your active line back into its starting point.

2.   Braiding - Whether it's a classic, braided or beaded bracelet, being able to do braids is important. It's a great way to start and end your bracelets to keep the strands or sections in order.

Braided bracelets are a delight as they are both visually appealing and quick to do. Once you master the different braiding techniques, you'll be rewarded with attractive accessories that are a breeze to make.

With this book you'll learn to do the following

a. 3 Strand Braiding Technique – Uses three strands or three sections to create a basic braid.

b. 4 Strand Braiding Technique – Uses four strands or sections to create a thicker braid.

c. 5 Strand Braiding Technique – Uses five
    strands to create a flat braid with a pattern
    that looks like a Celtic knot.

d. 6 strand braiding technique – Uses six
    strands or sections to create either a round
    or flat braid. This type of braid works
    better with thicker or wider strands such
    as Para cords or braided thread.

Chapter 3 – Classic Friendship Bracelets

Two Strand Chain Basic Bracelet

This is a great project to get you started as it will help you practice the basic forward knot. And because the steps involved in completing this bracelet is so easy, you'll have it completed in no time.

Difficulty Level: *Easy*

Materials:

- *2 Different Shades of Embroidery Floss or Thread*
- *Scissors*
- *Masking Tape*

Steps:

1.	Measure the length of your floss by holding out the end of the strand from your left hand to your right shoulder. If you want a thicker bracelet then you'll need about three strands for each floss color.

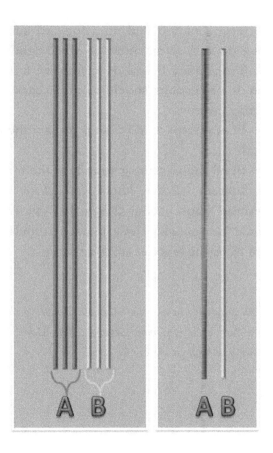

2.	Gather all the strands and create an overhead knot about 5 inches from the end of the strands.

3.	Arrange the strands and divide it into two so that all the strands of the same color are in the same section. The color on the left will be labeled A while the color on the right will be labeled B.

4.	Tape the strands down on the table or a clipboard to keep them in place.

5.	Take Color A and do a forward knot. After this is done, A should now be on the right.

6.	Take Color B and do a forward knot. Your strands or sections should now be back in their starting position.

7.	Repeat steps 4 and 5 until you get the desired length.

8.	Braid the remaining strands at the top and at the bottom of the knots and close with an overhead knot. About 2-3 inches on each end should be enough. These braided strands can be used to tie the bracelet around the wrist.

Note: You may need to tape the completed length to the table or your workspace as it may move around a bit. More strands for each section will create a thicker bracelet.

CANDY CANE STRIPES

This charming pattern is made up of narrow stripes that look quite dainty. It is a quick project to finish so you enjoy wearing it or giving it to your friends without spending too much time completing it. The guide below is for a narrow bracelet about 2-3 cm's wide.

Difficulty Level: ***Beginner***

Materials:

- *4 strands of embroidery floss.*
- *Scissors*
- *Masking Tape*

Steps:

1. Measure the length of the strands that you will be using by holding the end of the thread from

your left hand to your right shoulder. You can choose 2-4 shades depending on the color pattern that you wish to get. See below for examples of patterns that can be formed.

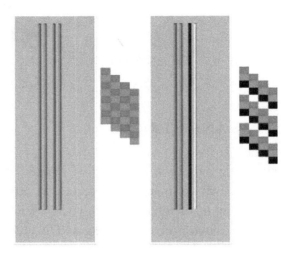

2.   Gather the strands together with an overhand knot about three inches from the end.

3.   Arrange the strands in the order that you want the stripes to appear. If you will be using just two shades, alternate the strands to create the narrow strips. If you want wider strips then position similar colored strands next to each other.

4.   The first strand will be A, the second B, the third C and the last D.

5.   Take A in your hand, this will be your active line. Do a forward knot on B twice.

6.   Continue doing 2 forward knots on the

remaining strands until you get to the end. The order of your strands will now be B, C, D and A.

7.   Take B in your hand, this will be your active line. Do a forward knot on C twice.

8.   Continue doing 2 forward knots on the remaining strands until you get to the end. The order of your strands should now be C, D, A and C.

9.   Take C in your hand, this is now your active line. Do 2 forward knots on D.

10.   Continue doing 2 forward knots on the remaining strands to the right until you get to the end. The order is now D. A, B and C.

11.   Take D in your hand, this is your active line. Do 2 forward knots on A.

12.   Continue doing the forward knots on the remaining strands until you get to the end. The order should be back to A, B, C and D.

13.   Repeat the steps until you get the length you want.

14.   Close the bracelet with an overhand knot. Leave about 3 inches of length lace it onto the wrist

Two Color Stripes

This charming pattern is made up of two contrasting or monochromatic shades. It is a classic design that you and your friends will certainly have fun making and wearing. It is similar to the candy stripes but the strips are just a bit wider. And because there are more strands or sections used, you'll get a much wider band around your wrist.

Difficulty Level: *Beginner*

Materials:

- *2 different embroidery floss or thread colors with 4 strands each*
- *Scissors*
- *Masking Tape*

Steps:

1. Measure the length of the strands by holding the end of each strand from your left hand to your right shoulder.
2. Gather the strands by making an overhand knot about three inches from the end.
3. See following illustration for the labels that will be used in the succeeding instructions.

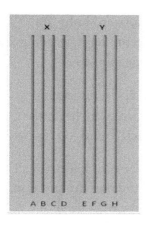

4.   Take Strand A from color X and do 2 forward knots on Strand B.

5.   Continue knotting on the remaining strands with Stand A serving as your active line. By the end of this step, the order of your strands will resemble what's shown below,

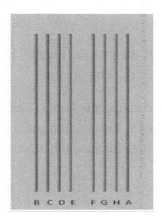

6. Take strand B and do 2 forward knots on Strand C. Continue moving to the right by doing 2 forward knots on the remaining strands.

7. Repeat the process with all the remaining strands, making sure that you keep the left most strand as the active line for each round.

8. Once you complete the forward knots for all the strands in Color X, you'll see that the position of the colors of the strands have now been reversed. Color X is now on the right while Color Y is on the left.

9. Take Strand E and do 2 forward knots on strand F. Make sure that your active line's color appears on top after each knot.

10. Continue doing the forward knots for all the remaining strands until strand E is at the right most side.

11. Repeat the process until all the strands are back in their starting position.

12. Keep making the knots until you get the desired length. You should get a pattern that resembles the illustration below.

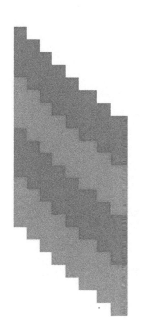

UNEVEN STRIPES

If you're looking for a variation to the stripes pattern then this is a great design to try out. It still uses just two colors but provides you with an alternative to the plain stripes. It is also quite easy to do.

The pattern below uses blue and orange. But you can substitute or replace this with any color that you want.

Difficulty Level: *Beginner*

Materials:

- *4 strands or sections of Color X (your choice of color)*
- *2 strands or sections of Color Y (your choice of color)*
- *Scissors*
- *Masking Tape*
- *Work area or Clipboard*

Steps:

1. Measure the length of the strands by holding the end of each strand from your left hand to your right shoulder.
2. Gather the strands by making an overhand knot about three inches from the end.
3. Arrange the strands as shown in the following illustration. The design of your bracelet is also shown in the same illustration.

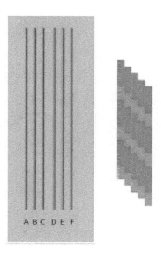

A B C D E F

4.   Tape down your strands to stop it from moving around too much while you make your knots.

5.   Take strand A, this will be your active line. Do 2 forward knots on strand B.

6.   Continue doing 2 forward knots on the remaining strands with stand A as your active line.

7.   Take strand B, this will now be your active line. Do 2 forward knots on strand C.

8.   Continue using strand B as your active line with the rest of the remaining strands.

9.   Repeat the process with the rest of the strands until you get the length you want.

CHEVRON

This pattern is your first step towards more complicated designs. The Chevron or V shaped pattern will let you practice the backward knot. While it may look a bit complex, it is quite easy to do.

Difficulty Level: **Advanced**

Materials:

- *2 strands or sections of Color X (your choice of color)*
- *2 strands or sections of Color Y (your choice of color)*
- *2 strands or sections of Color Z (your choice of color)*
- *Scissors*
- *Masking Tape*
- *Work area or Clipboard*

Steps:

1. Measure the length of the strands by holding the end of each strand from your left hand to your right shoulder.

2. Gather the strands by making an overhand knot about three inches from the end.

3. Arrange the strands in mirror image as shown in the following illustration. The design of your bracelet is also shown in the same illustration.

4. Tape down the strands onto your work table or clipboard to keep them in place.

5.   Take strand A as your active line. Do 2 forward knots on strand B.

6.   With strand A still as your active line do 2 forward knots on strand C.

7.   Take strand F as your active line and do 2 backward knots on strand E.

8.   With strand F still as your active line, do 2 backward knots on strand D.

9.   To complete the V shape, take strand F and do 2 backward knots on strand A. The order of your strands should now be B, C, F, A, D and E.

10.   Take strand B as your active line and do 2 forward knots on strand C.

11.   With strand B still as your active line, do 2 forward knots on strand F which moved from the right most earlier.

12.   Take strand E as your active line and do 2 backward knots on strand D.

13.   With strand E still as an active line, do 2 backward knots on strand A.

14.   To complete the V, take strand E and do 2 backward knots on strand B. The order of your strands should now be C, F, E, B, A and D

15.   Take strand C as your active line and do 2 forward knots on strand F.

16.   With strand C still as your active line, do 2 forward knots on strand E.

17.   Take strand D as your active line and do 2 backward knots on strand A.

18.   With strand D still as your active line, do 2 backward knots on strand B.

19.   To complete the V shape, take strand D and do 2 backward knots on strand C.

20.   With the first round done, the colors of your strands should be similar to what it was when you started.

21.   Repeat the process until you get the length that you need.

BASIC DIAMOND PATTERN

This pattern uses all the knots, the forward, backward, forward-backward and backward-forward. Working on this design may take a bit longer but the end product is a beautiful bracelet that you and your friends will love.

Difficulty Level: *Intermediate*

Materials:

- *4 strands or sections of Color X (your choice of color)*
- *2 strands or sections of Color Y (your choice of color)*
- *2 strands or sections of Color Z (your choice of color)*
- *Scissors*
- *Masking Tape*
- *Work area or Clipboard*

Steps:

1. Measure the length of the strands by holding the end of each strand from your left hand to your right shoulder.
2. Gather the strands by making an overhand knot about three inches from the end.
3. Arrange the strands in mirror image as shown in the following illustration. The design of your bracelet is also shown in the same illustration.

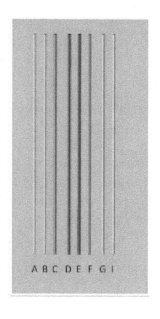

A B C D E F G I

4.   Take strand B as your active line and do 2 backward knots on strand A.

5.   Take Strand D as your active line and do 2 backward knots on strand C.

6.   Take strand as your active line and do 2 forward knots on strand F.

7.   Take strand G as your active line and do 2 forward knots on strand I.

8.   Take strand D as your active line and do 2 backward knots on strand A.

9.   Take strand C as your active line and do 2

forward knots on strand F.

10.   Take strand E as your active line and do 2 forward knots on strand I.

11.   Take strand D as your active line and do 2 backward-forward knots on strand B.

12.   Take strand F as your active line and do 2 backward-forward knots on strand A.

13.   Take strand C as your active line and do 2 forward backward knots on strand I.

14.   Take strand D as your active line and do 2 forward knots on strand A.

15.   Take strand F as your active line and do 2 forward knots on strand C.

16.   Take strand E as your active line and do 2 backward knots on strand I.

17.   Take strand B and do 2 forward-backward knots on strand A.

18.   Take strand D as your active line and do 2 forward knots on strand C.

19.   Take strand E as your active line and do 2 backward knots on strand F.

20.   Take strand I as your active line and do 2 backward-forward knots on strand G.

21.   Take strand A as your active line and do 2 forward-backward knots on strand C.

22.   Take strand E as your active line and do 2 backward knots on strand D.

23.   Take strand I as your active line and do 2 backward-forward knots on strand F.

24.   Relabel your strands back to A, B, C, D, E, F, G and H according to their current order,

25.   Repeat steps 4 to 24 until you get the length you want.

BASIC ZIGZAG

This pattern looks really cool with a strip of color zigzagging through your bracelet. It is easy to do because of the repeating pattern.

For this design, you'll need two different shades of thread or floss.

Difficulty Level: *Advanced*

Materials:

- *5 strands or sections of Color X (your choice of color)*
- *1 strand or section of Color Y (your choice of color)*
- *Scissors*
- *Masking Tape*
- *Work area or Clipboard*

Steps:

1. Measure the length of the strands by holding the end of each strand from your left hand to your right shoulder.
2. Gather the strands by making an overhand knot about three inches from the end.
3. Arrange the strands as shown in the following illustration. The design of your bracelet is also shown in the same illustration.

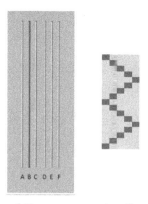

A B C D E F

5.　　　Take Strand B as your active line and do two backward-forward knots on strand A.

6.　　　Take strand C as your active line and do 2 forward knots on strand D.

7.　　　Take strand E as your active line and do 2 forward knots on strand F.

8.　　　Take strand B as your active line and do 2 forward knots on strand D.

9.　　　Take strand C as your active line and do 2 forward knots on strand F

10.　　Take strand A which is at the leftmost side as your active line and do 2 forward knots on strand D

11.　　Take strand B as your active line and do 2 forward knots on strand F.

12.   Take strand C as your active line and do 2 forward knots on strand E.

13.   Take strand A as your active line and do 2 forward knots on strand F.

14.   Take strand B as your active line and do 2 forward knots on strand E.

15.   Take strand F as your active line and do 2 forward knots on strand D.

16.   Take strand A as your active line and do 2 forward knots on strand E.

17.   Take strand B and do 2 forward-backward knots on strand C.

18.   Take strand D as your active line and do 2 forward knots on strand E.

19.   Take strand B as your active line and do 2 backward knots on strand A.

20.   Take strand F as your active line and do 2 forward knots on strand E located on its right side.

21.   Take strand B, the only different colored strand and do 2 backward knots on strand D which is to its left.

22.   Take strand A as your active line and do 2 forward knots on strand C.

23.   Take strand B as your active line and do 2 backward knots on strand F.

24.   Take Strand D as your active line and do 2 forward knots on strand C.

25.   The order of the strands is now E, B, F, C, D and A. Relabel the strands back to A, B, C, D, E and F.

26.   Repeat steps 5- 25 until you get the length you need.

HORIZONTAL TWO TONE PATTERN

This simple design is a joy to create because of the repetitive steps needed in the pattern. It's a quick project that needs only 9 strands.

Difficulty Level: ***Beginner***

Materials:

- *5 strands or sections of Color X (your choice of color)*
- *4 strands or sections of Color Y (your choice of color)*
- *Scissors*
- *Masking Tape*
- *Work area or Clipboard*

Steps:

1. Measure the length of the strands by holding the end of each strand from your left hand to your right shoulder.
2. Gather the strands by making an overhand knot about three inches from the end.
3. Arrange the strands as shown in the following illustration. The design of your bracelet is also shown in the same illustration.

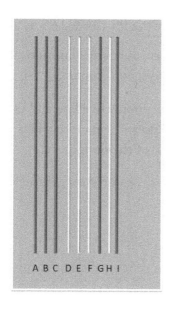

A B C D E F G H I

4.   Take strand A as your active string and do 2 forward-backward knots on strand B.

5.   Take strand D as your active line and do 2 backward-forward knots on strand C.

6.   Take strand F as your active line and do 2 backward-forward knots on strand E.

7.   Take strand G as your active line and do 2 forward-backward knots on strand H. This will complete the first row of knots for the pattern.

8.   Take strand B and do 2 forward-backward knots on strand C.

9.   Take strand E as your active line and do 2

45

backward-forward knots on strand D.

10.　　Take strand F as your active line and do 2 forward-backward knots on strand G.

11.　　Take strand I as your active line and do 2 backward-forward knots on strand H. This will complete the 2nd row of the design.

12.　　Repeat steps 4 to 11 until you get the length you want.

HEART

This charming pattern is sure to be a hit among your friends. Whether it's for Valentine's Day or simply a pattern you like, this heart design is a project that you will enjoy completing.

The pattern only needs 8 strands and 2 different shades so it's not a confusing design to work on.

Difficulty Level: ***Advanced***

Materials:

- *4 strands or sections of Color X (your choice of color)*
- *4 strands or sections of Color Y (your choice of color)*
- *Scissors*
- *Masking Tape*
- *Work area or Clipboard*

Steps:

1.   Measure the length of the strands by holding the end of each strand from your left hand to your right shoulder.
2.   Gather the strands by making an overhand knot about three inches from the end.
3.   Arrange the strands as shown in the following illustration. The design of your bracelet is also shown in the same illustration.

4.   Tape the strands down on your work table or a clipboard to keep them in place while knotting.

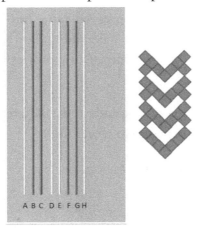

5.   Take strand B as your active line and do 2 backward knots on strand A. This should move Strand B to the left most side.

6.   Take strand C as your active line and do 2 forward knots on strand D.

7.   Take strand F as your active line and do 2 backward knots on strand E.

8.   Take strand G as your active line and do 2 forward knots on strand H.

9.   At the end of these series of knots, your strands should be in this order, B, A, D, C, F, E, G and H. Using the colors in the illustration earlier, the color sequence should now be,

Blue- white –white –blue-blue-white-white-blue

10. For the next row, take strand A (white) as your active line and do 2 forward knots on strand D (white).

11. Take strand C (blue) as your active line and do 2 forward knots on strand F (blue).

12. Take strand E (white) as your active line and do 2 forward knots on strand G (blue)

13. At the end of these 2nd series of knots, the order of your strands should be,

B-D-A-F-C-G-E-H

The color sequence based on the colors in the illustration should be,

Blue-white-white-blue-blue-white-white-blue

14. For the next row of knots, take strand B (blue) as your active strand and do 2 forward knots on strand D (white).

15. Take strand A (white) as your active line and do 2 forward knots on strand F (blue).

16. Take strand H (white) as your active line and do 2 backward knots on strand C (white).

17. Take strand G(blue) as your active line and do 2 backward knots on strand E (white)

18.   After the 3rd series of knots, the order of your strands should be as shown below,

D-B-F-A-H-C-G-E

19.   For the next row of knots, take strand B (blue) as your active string and do 2 forward knots on strand F (blue) which is directly to its right.

20.   Take strand A (white) as your active line and do 2 forward knots on the strand to its right which is strand H (white).

21.   Take strand D(blue) as your active line and do 2 forward knots on strand G (blue)

22.   At the end of the 4th series of knots, the order of your strands should be as follows,

D-F-B-H-A-G-C-E

The color series should be as follows,

White-blue-blue-white-white-blue-blue-white

23.   Relabel your strands back to A-B-C-D-E-F-G-H- and repeat the row knotting steps above until you get the desired length.

CHAPTER 4 – WRAPPED FRIENDSHIP BRACELETS

ONE-COLOR WRAPPED FRIENDSHIP BRACELET

The basic single color wrapped bracelet is a great project to start with. It gives you the chance to practice the basic knots and wrapping technique that you will need to be able to create more complex patterns.

Difficulty Level: *Easy*

Materials:

- *14strands of floss or thread in the same color about 30 inches long each*
- *Scissors*
- *Masking Tape*
- *clipboard*

Steps:

1. Gather your strands together by making an overhand knot about 4-5 inches from the end. Tape the strands down on your work table or clipboard.

2. Pick one of the strings which will be your wrapping line.

3. Take your wrapping line and do a forward knot over the remaining 13 strands. This will keep the strands in place and prevent your wrapping line from unraveling.

4. Wrap all the strands snugly with the wrapping line, making sure that none of the standing strands are left uncovered.

5. Continue wrapping until you get about an inch of wrapped thread or floss. Take your wrapping line and do a forward knot to keep the wrap in place.

6.   Take another strand (different from the first one) and use this as your new wrapping line.

7.   With your new wrapping line, do a forward knot around the rest of the strands.

8.   Repeat steps 4-7 until you get the length that you need. Remember to change wrapping lines after about an inch of wrap to avoid any unraveling of the thread or floss.

9.   Once you get the length you want, do 2 forward knots with your wrapping line.

10.   Seal the wrap with an overhand knot.

STRIPED WRAPPED FRIENDSHIP BRACELET

With the basics of the wrapped bracelet under your belt, you can now start creating more colorful projects. The Striped pattern lets you combine different shades into one bracelet. You can create a rainbow of colors in just one bracelet.

Difficulty Level: *Easy*

Materials:

- *14strands of floss or thread in colors you want with about 30 inches in length. (You can use more strands if you want a thicker bracelet.*
- *Scissors*
- *Masking Tape*
- *clipboard*

Steps:

1. Gather your strands together by making an overhand knot about 4-5 inches from the end. Tape the strands down on your work table or clipboard.

2. Choose a strand of the color that you want to start with and pull it apart from the rest of the threads. This will be your wrapping line.

3. Take your wrapping line and do a forward

knot on the other threads. This knot will keep the standing lines in place so you can easily do your wrapping.

4. Wrap the wrapping line around the rest of the strands snugly. Make sure that none of the standing lines show through the wrap.

5. Keep wrapping until you get about ¾ of an inch. Take your wrapping line and do a forward knot on the standing strands.

6. Take a strand of the next color you want to use and set it aside. This will be your new wrapping line.

7. With your new wrapping line, make a forward knot on the rest of the strands. Push the knot snugly into the forward knot from your first wrapping line.

8. Repeat Steps 4-7 until you use all the colors you want and get the desired length.

9. To seal the wrap, do an overhand knot it push it tightly against the last forward knot.

CRISSCROSSED FRIENDSHIP BRACELET

This pattern adds a crisscross design to your bracelet. It gives your accessory an interesting texture as well as an additional splash of color.

Difficulty Level: Advanced

Materials:

- *14 strands of floss or thread in colors you want to use measuring about 30 inches long.*
- *Scissors*
- *Masking Tape*
- *clipboard*

Steps:

1.   Gather your strands together by making an overhand knot about 4-5 inches from the end. Tape the strands down on your work table or clipboard.

2.   Take a strand of the color you wish to use and set it aside. This will be you wrapping line.

3.   Take 2 more strands in the colors you want to use and set these aside. These will be your crisscross lines.

4.   Take your wrapping line and do a forward knot on the remaining 11 strands. Make sure

you're crisscross lines are not included.

5. Wrap the strands with your wrapping line as snugly as you can. Make sure that none of the strands being wrapped shows through.

6. Once you get about an inch of wrap, do a forward knot with your wrapping line over the 11 standing strands. This will make sure that your wrap stays in place.

7. Take your crisscross lines and tightly crisscross them around the wrapped strands.

8. Pinch the end of your crisscross lines and choose a new wrapping line and 2 new crisscross lines.

9. Take your new wrapping line and do a forward knot on the strands. Make sure that your new crisscross lines are not included.

10. Repeat steps 5-9 until you use all the colors you want and the length you need.

11. Seal the wraps with an overhand knot pushed snugly against the last forward knot.

FISHTAIL FRIENDSHIP BRACELET

The fishtail pattern has an interesting design that looks a lot harder to make that it actually is. It works best with thicker yarn or even cords. However, multiple strands of embroidery thread or floss can create the same fishtail effect as well.

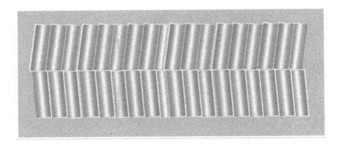

Difficulty Level: Advanced

Materials:

- 3 strands of thread or floss in any color about 60 inches long.
- 1 strand of yellow thread about 60 inches long
- 1 strand of green thread about 60 inches long
- 1 strand of red thread about 60 inches long
- Scissors
- Masking Tape
- clipboard

Steps:

1. Take the 3 strands of thread in the same color and fold it in half so you get 6 strands that are 30 inches long. These will be your standing strands.

2. On the end with the loops, make an overhand knot about 3-4 inches from the loops.

3. Take the yellow, green and red threads and gather them together. Fold them in half so you now have 6 strands of thread that are about 30 inches long. The multi colored strands will serve as your active lines.

4. Divide the active lines into 2. The left side will be A while the right will be labeled B as shown in the illustration below.

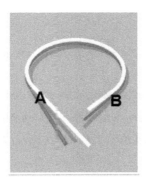

5.   Take your standing strands and separate it
        into two sections. Label the left side as X and
        the right side Y as shown in the illustration
        below.

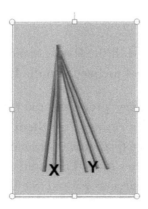

6.   Take your active lines and put it around your
        standing strands as shown in the following
        illustration.

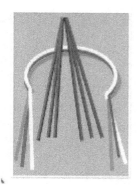

7.   Take section A and cross it over X and then under Y.

8.   Take section B and cross it over Y and then under X.

9.   Pull the loops you'd created tight. Make sure that the active strands are completely covering your standing strands.

10.   Take Section B and cross it over X and then under Y.

11.   Take section A and cross it over Y and then under X.

12.   Pull the loops tight.

13.   Repeat steps 7-12 until you get the length you need.

14.   Close the wrap with an overhand knot.

KNOTTED AND WRAPPED FRIENDSHIP BRACELET

This pattern uses knots to wrap around the standing lines. The result is an interesting design that looks quite sturdy. It is the perfect friendship bracelet for your male friends as the design is similar to that of paracord bracelets.

The pattern below uses blue and brown thread. However, you can replace it with any other shades that you may prefer to use.

Difficulty Level: Advanced

Materials:

- *3 strands of brown thread or floss about 60 inches long.*
- *3 strands of brown thread or floss about 30 inches long.*
- *3 strands of blue thread or floss about 60 inches long.*
- *3 strands of blue thread or floss about 30 inches long.*
- *Scissors*
- *Masking Tape*
- *clipboard*

Steps:

1.   Gather all your threads together by making an overhand knot.

2.	Arrange your thread so that the colors are alternating with the shorter strands in the middle. Your strands should be arranged as shown in the following illustration.

3.	Anchor your strands by taping or hooking them down.

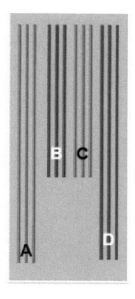

4.	Take strands D as your active line and cross over and under strands C. Pull the strands through the loop and tighten the knot.

5.	With strands D still as your active line cross under and over strands C. Pull D through the loop and tighten the knot.

6. Take strands A as your active line and cross over and under strands B. Pull the strands through the loop and tighten the knot.

7. Repeat steps 4-6 until you get the length you want.

8. Seal the pattern by gathering all the strands in an overhand knot.

LADDER WRAP FRIENDSHIP BRACELET

This patterns is quite popular but is often made from thicker materials such as nylon cords. However, multiple strands of embroidery floss will produce great results as well.

Difficulty Level: Advanced

Materials:

- *3 strands of brown thread or floss about 60 inches long.*
- *3 strands of brown thread or floss about 30 inches long.*
- *3 strands of blue thread or floss about 60 inches long.*
- *3 strands of blue thread or floss about 30 inches long.*
- *Scissors*
- *Masking Tape*
- *clipboard*

Steps:

1.   Gather all your threads together by making an overhand knot.

2.   Arrange your thread so that the colors are alternating with the shorter strands in the middle. Your strands should be arranged as shown in the following illustration.

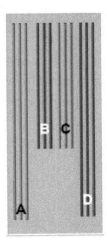

3. Take section A and create a loop with your forefinger. Leave the loop for later.

4. Cross section A over B and C. Do not tighten the strands.

5. Take section D and cross it over section A and then under C and B.

6. Push the strands of section D into the loop you made with the strands of section A.

7. Pull section D and section A to tighten the strands and create the knot that will wrap around sections B and C.

8. Take section A which is now located at the right most side and create a loop with your forefinger. Leave the loop for later.

9.   Cross section A over C and B. Just like before do not tighten or pull the strands.

10.   Take section D and cross it over section A and then under B and C.

11.   Push the strands of section D into the loop you made with the strands of section A.

12.   Tighten the knot by pulling sections A and D towards opposite directions. You can push the knot upwards to make it fit snugly against the earlier knot.

13.   With the sections back in the original order, simply repeat steps 3-12 until you get the length you want.

Chapter 6 – Braided Friendship Bracelets

Three Strand Flat Braid Friendship Bracelet

This is the most basic braiding style which means it is also the easiest to do. It is a quick project so you can get it finished in no time. You can also use this type of braid to clean up the strands for any of your friendship bracelets.

Difficulty Level: Beginner

Materials:

- *3 strands of yellow thread*
- *3 strands of red thread*
- *3 strands of blue thread*
- *Scissors*
- *Masking Tape*
- *clipboard*

Steps:

1.   Gather all the strands together with an overhand knot.

2.   Arrange the strands in the order that you want. If you a tie dye effect. you can put one strand of each color in each section.

3.   Take strands or section A and cross it over section B. Section A will now be your middle strands.

4.   Take strands or section C and cross it over section A.

5.   The order of the sections will now be B-C-A. Relabel your sections back to A-B-C.

6.   Repeat steps 3-5 until you get the length you need.

7.   Seal the braid to avoid any unravelling by doing an overhand knot and push it tightly against the end of the braid.

FOUR STRAND ROPE BRAID FRIENDSHIP BRACELET

This is a rather complex braiding technique that will take a bit to master. The steps are a bit confusing but once you get the hang of it, you'll be rewarded with a beautiful braid that makes a great bracelet.

Difficulty Level: Advanced

Materials:

- *3 strands of yellow thread*
- *3 strands of red thread*
- *3 strands of blue thread*
- *3 strands of green thread*
- *Scissors*
- *Masking Tape*
- *clipboard*

Steps:

1. Gather all the strands together with an overhand knot.

2. Anchor your threads with tape or a pin.

3. Label your strands/sections so that you can easily keep track of which is which. In this braid, the first strand will be A, the 2nd B, the

3rdC3 and the last D.

4. The order of your strands as well as the pattern it will create is shown in the following illustration.

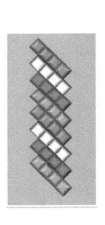
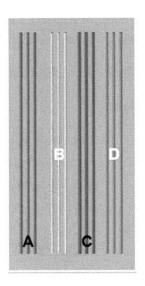

5. Take strand/section D as your active strands and cross it over B and C. The order of your strands will now be A, D, B and C.

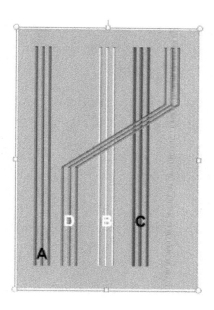

6.   Take strand/section B and cross it over D. The order now is A, B, D and C.

7.   Take strand/section A and cross it over B and D. The strands/sections are now arranged as B, D, A and C.

8.   Take strand/section A and cross it over D. The order of your strands is now B, A, D and C.

9.   Tighten the braid by pulling the strands up and then to the side.

10.   Take strand/section C and cross it over D and A. The strands should now be arranged as B, C, A and D.

11. Take strand/section A and cross it over C. You should now have the strands in the following order B, A, C and D.

12. Take strand/section B and cross it over A and C. The order is now A, C, B and D.

13. Take strand/section C and cross it over B. You should now be back to the order A, B, C and D.

14. Repeat the steps until you get the length you want.

FIVE STRAND FLAT BRAID FRIENDSHIP BRACELET

This braid when finished looks a lot like a Celtic knot. The steps are easy but mastering the braid may take a while as it is a bit difficult to tighten the strands.

You can replace the recommended colors used in the pattern with shades that you prefer.

Difficulty Level: Advanced

Materials:

- *15 strands of embroidery floss or thread*
- *Scissors*
- *Masking Tape*
- *clipboard*

Steps:

1.	Gather all the strands together with an overhand knot.

2.	Anchor your threads with tape or a pin.

3.	Divide your thread in 5 sections. Each section should have 3 strands.

4.	Label each section as shown in the illustration below.

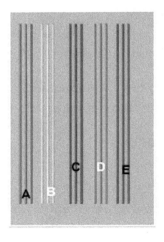

5.	Take section B as your active strands and cross it over section C.

6.	Take section D and cross it over section B. The order of your strands should now be A-C-D-B-E

7.   Take Section C and cross it over section A.

8.   Take section B and cross it over section E. Pull the threads to tighten the braid. The order of your strands should now be C-A-D-E-B.

9.   Relabel your sections back to A-B-C-D-E.

10.   Repeat the steps 5-9 until you get the length you want.

11.   Seal the braid with an overhand knot.

SIX STRAND ROUND BRAID FRIENDSHIP BRACELET

This braid is a chunkier and sturdier version of the 4 strand round braid. While it may look complicated, it is quite easy to do as the steps are not hard to follow

Difficulty Level: Advanced

Materials:

- *18 strands of embroidery floss or thread*
- *Scissors*
- *Masking Tape*
- *clipboard*

Steps:

1.   Gather all the strands together with an overhand knot.

2.   Anchor your threads with tape or a pin.

3.   Divide the strands into 6 sections. Each section should have three strands. If you are using cords or a thicker yarn, you may need to use less strands.

4.   Label each section as shown in the following illustration

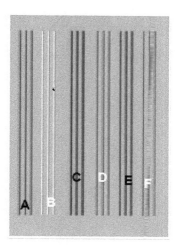

5.	Separate the sections into 2 parts. Take A-B-C, this will be the left strands. The D-E-F will be the right strands. Each side will always have all the same strands after each weave.

6.	Take section A and cross it under sections B, C, D, E and F.

7.	With section A still as your active line, cross it over F, under E, over D. The order of your strands will now be B-C-A-D-E-F

8.	Take section or strands F and cross it under all strands until it is below B.

9.	With section F still as your active line, cross it over B, under C and over A. Pull section F towards the right side. The order of your strands should now be B-C-A-F-D-E.

10. Relabel your strands back to A-B-C-D-E-F.

11. Repeat steps 6-10 until you get the length you want.

CHAPTER 7 – TIPS ON MAKING FRIENDSHIP BRACELETS

Making your own bracelets to wear or share with your friends is a lot of fun. There's nothing more fulfilling than to see patterns being created from a handful of thread.

Below are some tips that you can use to make the experience more enjoyable.

Tip #1 – Keep your materials and equipment organized

Whether you're planning on making one or one hundred bracelets, it's important to make sure that you have everything you need ready. The perfect solution is to have a box or kit where you can keep all your materials in order. With a neat bracelet kit, you'll always feel excited about working on your bracelets.

1. Embroidery Thread – When new, embroidery thread is coiled neatly so it's easy to store. However, once it has been used, the remaining strands can easily get tangled. To avoid this, you can use cardboard tubes to stay organized. Wind the strands around the tube and tape the loose ends to prevent them from unravelling when not in use.

If you don't have any cardboard tubes available, you can use wooden clothespins instead. Just upon the clothespin and place one end of the strand. This will make it easier for you to wind the strand around the clothespin. Simply slip the other end through the clothespin to keep it from unravelling.

You can label the clothespin so you know the exact shade of the embroidery floss. This will come in really handy when you need to purchase more thread of that color.

Place the wound up strands in clear plastic bags so you can easily see the colors. This way, you won't need to dig through the thread and end up unwinding and tangling the strands.

Keeping your thread neat and in order will make it easier for you to find what you need when you start working on a project.

2.   Beads and Buttons – Beads and buttons are a great way to embellish your bracelets. They can easily be weaved into the patterns. You can also use these as clasps. So, it would be ideal to have these stored along with your other friendship bracelet supplies.

You can use clear mason jars for bigger beads and buttons. You can easily see what's in the jar so you won't need to pour everything out when looking for a specific bead or button.

For smaller beads and buttons, you can use medicine bottles or even an ice cube tray. Aside from organizing by size, you may also want to segregate them by color so you can quickly match the perfect bead or button with the thread or floss you will be using.

3. Scissors – This is an absolute must in your craft kit. You'll need a sharp pair that can easily and neatly snip your thread and other materials that may need cutting.

    When storing your crafting shears, put it in a case or small box to avoid any accidents. The sharp point should always be pointed downwards if you will be storing it upright. Also, make sure you don't store damp scissors as these may result in rusting.

4. Other Necessities – Other things that you want to make sure you have in your kit are the following,

    a. Safety Pins – These will come in handy when you're knotting and braiding. You can pin the strands onto a surface to prevent it from twisting and turning which may make it difficult for you to knot or braid.

Safety Pins are also practical to have around as you can easily unravel any knots made in error without much problem.

b. Masking Tape – When working on a hard flat surface, you might not have anywhere to pin your project on to keep it in place. Using tape to keep it down is a great alternative. This is also ideal for when you've knotted or braided quite a length so you can keep the bracelet flat and easy to work on.

c. Clipboard – This equipment is a cost effective alternative to crafting boards. These can easily be bought at most shops at a cheap price. The clip can anchor your strand, while the board can give you a flat surface to work on.

You can store these equipment and materials in smaller boxes that can fit into your bigger kit.

Tip # 2 – Start with the Basics

With so many cool patterns to choose from, you may be tempted to take on complex designs. While there is certainly nothing wrong with taking on a challenge, you may want to start off with simpler designs.

Working on more intricate patterns too soon may result in

some confusion. You might get lost with all the knots or braids and you may end up getting frustrated. This might result in you not finishing your project or giving up on making friendship bracelets.

Pick patterns that you can finish in minutes so that you can quickly see the results. Seeing completed bracelets will inspire you to continue working on more fun and colourful accessories to wear or give to friends.

So, while you're gusto and enthusiasm is a great start, put off working on patterns with dozens of strands until you're more comfortable reading patterns, tying knots and braiding braids.

Tip # 3 – Practice

There are 4 different types of knots used in making friendship bracelets. Some patterns require that you use all of them while others don't. So, to be able to make more intricate designs, you'll need to be able to do all 4 knots.

Practice these knots on spare strands to become more comfortable with the steps on how these are done. When you do this, you'll find yourself completing projects a lot faster. You'll see that you're hands will be moving almost on auto-pilot once you've mastered the knots and braids.

Tip # 4 – Don't be Afraid to Experiment

Friendship Bracelets are fun and colourful accessories. While the patterns included in this book have recommended colors, go ahead and try out different shades when making your bracelets. Use colors that represent you and your friends to make these accessories more personal.

Also, when you start getting used to the basic patterns, you can start experimenting on your own. You can start creating designs from simply changing a step or two in the patterns included in this guide. The worst thing that can happen is that you might need to unravel some knots or braids.

Taking the risk when it comes to colors and patterns may result in eye catching beautiful friendship bracelets that your friends are going to adore wearing.

Tip # 5 – Celebrate Your Projects

No matter how simple you think the pattern is, a completed bracelet is certainly something to celebrate. Whether you made it for yourself or those close to you take time to enjoy your handiwork and take pride in what you've completed.

Even if your bracelet does not look exactly like what the patterns say they should look like, it is still a handmade accessory filled with hours of love and hard work. Besides, think of it not as failing to copy a pattern but rather a successful endeavour in creating a new design.

CONCLUSION:

I hope you enjoyed the patterns included in this book. From classic knotted friendship bracelets to hippie wraps and braids, you'll spend hours working on projects that's guaranteed to make you and your friends smile.

The next step is to embrace the beautiful tradition of friendship bracelets and start working on projects that symbolize your special relationship with the folks around you. Whether you are an expert on macramé and weaving or just a greenhorn trying out your hand at this craft, you'll certainly find something perfect in the included designs.

So, take your embroidery thread or floss out and start flexing your fingers. Knot and braid while watching your favourite show or listening to music. Where ever and whenever you want to start knotting and braiding, this book will help you make charming bracelets to wear and share.

CPSIA information can be obtained
at www.ICGtesting.com
Printed in the USA
BVHW041911260220
573424BV00009B/325